Meeting the Challenges:
Developing Faculty Careers

by Michael C. T. Brookes
and Katherine L. German

ASHE-ERIC Higher Education Research Report No. 3, 1983

Prepared by

ERIC ®*Clearinghouse on Higher Education*
The George Washington University

Published by

ASHE

Association for the Study of Higher Education

Jonathan D. Fife,
Series Editor

Cite as:
Brookes, Michael C. T.; and German, Katherine L. *Meeting the Challenges: Developing Faculty Careers*. ASHE-ERIC Higher Education Research Report No. 3. Washington, D.C.: Association for the Study of Higher Education, 1983.

The ERIC Clearinghouse on Higher Education invites individuals to submit proposals for writing monographs for the Higher Education Research Report series. Proposals must include:
1. A detailed manuscript proposal of not more than five pages.
2. A 75-word summary to be used by several review committees for the initial screening and rating of each proposal.
3. A vita.
4. A writing sample.

ISSN 0737-1292
ISBN 0-913317-02-0

ERIC® Clearinghouse on Higher Education
The George Washington University
One Dupont Circle, Suite 630
Washington, D.C. 20036

Association for the Study of Higher Education
One Dupont Circle, Suite 630
Washington, D.C. 20036

This publication was prepared with funding from the National Institute of Education, U.S. Department of Education, under contract no. 400-82-0011. The opinions expressed in this report do not necessarily reflect the positions or policies of NIE or the Department.

CONTENTS

Executive Summary	1
What Changes Are Affecting Higher Education?	1
How Can Faculty Be Helped?	2
What's Special About Academic Careers?	2
Where Does Faculty Development Fit In?	3
What Lies Ahead?	4
An Age in Transition	6
Social Transition	6
Transition in Education	7
Professional Transition	9
Adult and Career Development	11
Adult Development	11
Career Development	14
Faculty Careers	17
The Faculty Role	18
Faculty Career Stages	20
Outcomes	24
Developing Solutions	27
Changing Role of Faculty Development	27
Faculty Development Programs	28
Faculty Career Development	31
Preparing for the Year 2,000	33
The Status Quo	33
The Dilemma of the Reward Structure	34
The Impact of Technology	36
Bibliography	38

FOREWORD

The essence of a higher education institution is the faculty. The sum of their training, values, behavior and morale, and their dedication to their profession and the institution dictates the quality and effectiveness of an institution. Failure to give careful consideration to the balancing of faculty expectations to institutional needs can be devastating. Because of the changing financial and enrollment conditions, institutions are finding it increasingly hard to provide a positive environment for faculty career development.

Faculty expectations are a product of the process of becoming and being a faculty member. Most faculty members move into their careers quite accidently, often because their success as undergraduates motivates them to pursue graduate training. As they succeed in graduate schools they increasingly accept the values and behavior patterns of their faculty role models and mentors. Positive experiences as research and teaching assistants further reinforce this process. The logical career step at graduation is to continue in academe by becoming part of the faculty. However, as they mature, their expectations, as well as institutional demands and their personal lives change.

Just as faculty expectations develop and change, so do institutional needs. During the past decade, institutions have experienced two primary changes that have particular meaning to faculty careers: a lessening of financial security and dramatic changes in the student body. In particular, today's students differ in three major ways from their predecessors in the 1950s and 1960s. First, there is an increasing number of college students with lower academic ability. Second, students' academic objectives are more influenced by long-term career objectives. And third, the majority of students in the 1980s are no longer the traditional 18–22-year-olds, but are instead more likely adults attending on a part-time basis.

There are noticeable consequences of these changes as faculty try to balance teaching and scholarship. Facing decreased financial support for research, fewer graduate and teaching assistants, and reduced support services (for secretarial services, photocopying and long-distance telephoning), faculty are finding it increasingly difficult to publish. As travel funds evaporate, they less frequently present papers at professional meetings and exchange ideas with colleagues. All this, added to salaries that have not kept pace with the changing economy, have taken their toll on faculty morale.

The changing pattern in student enrollment has necessitated changes in teaching patterns. Many students need developmental or remedial instruction. Adult and part-time students respond differently than younger full-time students, and demand different emphases than do more academically oriented students. Most faculty, trained in traditional graduate schools, are ill-equipped to accommodate these changes.

The ability of an institution to accommodate faculty expectations while meeting its own changing needs is of great importance. In this report, Michael C. T. Brookes, Dean of Academic Affairs at Queensborough Community College of the City University of New York, and Katherine L. German, Assistant Dean of Academic Affairs at North Shore Community College, analyze the literature encompassing this issue. Through their analysis of the basis of faculty expectations and the importance of considering the research in adult and career development, they provide permanent ways for institutions to develop a more positive atmosphere for their faculty.

Jonathan D. Fife
Director and Series Editor
ERIC* Clearinghouse on Higher Education
The George Washington University

EXECUTIVE SUMMARY

What Changes Are Affecting Higher Education?
Once again, American society finds itself in transition. The nation's social, economic, and political values are being transformed as we prepare for a postindustrial future very different from the industrial past that propelled the United States to a position of world leadership and economic dominance.

The changes of the past 20 years go much deeper than finances. Virtually every aspect of our national life, from defense to social security, is being questioned. Naturally, education is not exempt. The long history of social support for education has given way to increasing criticism. It is suggested that educators don't know what they are doing or that they are failing either to do what they should be doing or to do what they claim to be doing. The back-to-basics movement is gaining strength, the public investment in education is declining, and educators are being expected to provide a quick fix for the many ills from which our society is currently suffering.

This devaluation of the educational enterprise has brought with it a concomitant reduction in the status of the teaching profession. Faculty members, who entered the profession under very different conditions, have watched their purchasing power shrink with each salary check. As they unionized to buttress their shrinking economic status, they discovered that they also were losing the esteem and social status that the professoriate had enjoyed since World War II. Educational institutions, responding to social, political, and economic challenges, are fighting for their own survival. Many have instituted industrial management systems and have increased demands on employee contribution, productivity, and commitment. These attempts to secure institutional vitality have compounded the morale problem facing the professoriate.

The severity of these blows to the morale and sense of well-being of the faculty has been increased by dramatic changes in faculty careers. Traditional academic rewards have been reduced, teaching loads have been increased, and departments and programs have been eliminated. Faculty are being asked to expand their roles into new disciplines and new activities. Junior faculty have little to look forward to, and senior faculty have begun to feel that they are perceived as obstacles and as an unwelcome burden on the institution's salary account.

These changes have resulted in widespread dismay, anger, confusion, and resentment. Colleges and universities can no longer afford to overlook the legitimate needs and hopes of faculty no matter how intense the struggle for institutional survival becomes. It is the faculty who shape the image and the future of their institutions. They are also central to the mission of the institution. It is, therefore, essential that their concerns be heard and addressed.

How Can Faculty Be Helped?

To understand the needs and hopes of the faculty better requires some familiarity with the current research on life cycles and career stages. Erikson (1950, 1978), Erikson and Erikson (1981), Levinson (1978), Sheehy (1977, 1981), and Gould (1978), among others, have demonstrated that psychosocial development and change continue throughout adulthood and into old age. This process has been charted as a series of distinct stages, each bringing its unique concerns, needs, and responsibilities. Thus, the ways in which faculty members can be helped will depend to a considerable extent on the stage of psychosocial development through which the individual is progressing.

Similarly, research on careers has demonstrated that careers, like individuals, move through a series of identifiable stages challenging the individual in different ways and producing new sets of needs. Super (1980), Hall (1976), Hall and Nougaim (1968), and others have elaborated these stages and the demands they produce. Ralph (1978), Hodgkinson (1974), Baldwin (1979), Brookes (1980), and others translate generic career development research specifically to the demands of faculty careers. Through an understanding of the specific issues they confront along their careers, faculty can be helped and their vitality and contribution maintained.

What's Special About Academic Careers?

The academic profession has a number of singular characteristics. Many faculty appear to drift into the profession rather than choosing it (Light, Marsden, and Carl 1973). Young academics soon discover that teaching is a very solitary activity, that the profession is not supportive of norms of sharing, and that they are offered little guidance, mentoring, or support. Studies of the academic culture suggest that it is not conducive to the continued growth and development of its professionals (see, for example, Freedman et al. 1979). Moreover, the preparation graduate students receive bears little resemblance to what most of them do as faculty members. The emphasis in graduate school is on research in a chosen field; teaching typically receives little attention. Similarly, the reward structure in higher education favors research and publication heavily and pays little more than lip-service to excellence in teaching (Ladd 1979, p. 5).

Perhaps as a result there appears to be ambivalence about academe's principal function: teaching. Faculty rarely discuss teaching—their own least of all—and are encouraged to pay homage to research and publication rather than to classroom activity (Light, Marsden, and Carl 1973; Tuckman 1979). Because no generally accepted norms for measuring effective teaching have yet been devised, it is hard to evaluate what goes on in the classroom. Thus, a faculty member is denied any objective, concrete evidence of having accomplished anything at all. Moreover, faculty face a career in which the basic enterprise is unchanging; what they do one year they can expect to continue to do with only minor changes for the foreseeable future.

There appears to be ambivalence about academe's principal function: teaching.

Where Does Faculty Development Fit In?

To help offset these negative factors, the profession has had a tradition of supporting individual faculty as they pursue their own scholarly interests. This tradition was radically altered over the past decade, primarily in response to the impact of the social revolution of the 1960's in higher education. Traditional curricula and teaching approaches were not responsive to the insistent demands of the new generation of college students. To help faculty, programs of faculty development were rapidly designed and implemented on hundreds of campuses. Rather than supporting individual scholarly enterprises, these new programs were aimed at "improving" whole groups of faculty by equipping them with new techniques for the classroom, new ways of designing curriculum, new systems of grading, and new course content. The research of Smith (1976), Centra (1978), Gaff (1975), and others examines the various types of faculty development programs that have evolved. However, faculty participation in established programs has been limited, and serious questions have been raised regarding their effectiveness. Results were never overwhelmingly impressive or enduring. The programs suffered from some of the same problems that education often suffers from: the results were hard to measure and difficult to evaluate.

Recently, another kind of faculty development has arisen: Faculty Career Development. The approach here is extremely pragmatic and includes refined linkages to faculty evaluation; faculty retraining in the new high-demand, high-technology disciplines; efforts to help faculty move out of teaching into the corporate world; and the spread of early retirement incentives. Clearly, this represents a kind of development, but it is not necessarily academic or scholarly development.

Although these new initiatives contain much that is commendable, they also raise questions about the future for academics and for academic careers. Some faculty have been forced to pursue their academic careers on a part-time basis, moving from institution to institution as positions arise. Some have opted to develop a second, external, career to supplement their income and also their need for continued growth. Others have simply given up, suppressing the values that led them to education and choosing instead to pursue another line of work. A few have elected to retire early.

What Lies Ahead?
A dynamic relationship exists between the development of individual faculty, the development of their careers, and the overall well-being of institutions of higher education. It is essential not to lose sight of this point as institutions struggle for survival because most institutions already have, by and large, the faculty they will have 20 years hence. This fact adds urgency to the importance of educators becoming more knowledgeable about adult development and career stages. With that knowledge they can help promote a climate in which the elements of community and diversity (Erikson and Erikson 1981) can thrive.

A reform of the academic reward system also is urgently needed. At present, there is little support for teaching faculty and little recognition of the importance of what goes on in the classroom (Ladd 1979). Faculty who want to get ahead have to depend either on publication or on a switch into a primarily administrative role (Tuckman 1979). Until the formal academic reward system gives equal weight to teaching, putting it on a par with publication and administration, it is hard to see where teaching faculty—and they are more than three quarters of all higher education faculty members (Ladd 1979)—will find the strength and support they must have in order to become and remain dynamic, involved, vital, and generative.

Higher education faces a particularly demanding span of years during which financial resources seem certain to continue to be limited. Simultaneously, all faculty and all institutions face the enormous challenges created by the technological explosion. There is no doubt that education will survive. The really interesting question is whether educators will merely hunker down, stubbornly maintaining as much as possible of the Golden Age of the fifties, or whether, through a greater awareness of adult development needs and potentialities, we will turn these challenges into an unequaled opportunity for refocusing, reshaping, and revitalizing the traditional pattern of faculty careers. That is the challenge offered by the present crisis.

AN AGE IN TRANSITION

"Teacher-watching" has been one of my main enjoyments over the years. . . . One of the things I learned very early is that students always recognize a good teacher. . . . When students say about a teacher, "We are learning a great deal," they can be trusted. They know. But I also learned that "teacher" is an elusive term. Or, rather, I learned that there is no one answer to the question: What makes the effective teacher? No two teachers, I found, do the same things. No two teachers behave the same way. What works for one teacher and makes him first-rate does not seem to work at all for another one—or is never used by another one. It was all very confusing—and still is (Drucker 1979, pp. 75–76).

For years, educational researchers have scrutinized classrooms and have examined instructional methodologies. More recently, they have attempted to elaborate the characteristics of effective teaching. And yet, despite the proliferation of studies, the central activity of the profession continues to defy definition. As a result, more often than not, effective teaching is simply accepted as a creative activity driven by the force of the individual's personality. Both the layman and the professional alike acknowledge that given basic competence in a discipline and in teaching skills, there is an idiosyncratic element to teaching that underpins the view that the teacher makes the difference.

Higher education is a labor-intensive enterprise. As such, it depends greatly on the quality of learning that its faculty provides. These individuals, both singly and collectively, play a central role in developing and maintaining a collegiate image and reputation, the two factors that speak most directly to institutional vitality. Given the challenges of the contemporary educational marketplace, it is essential that educators reassess not only the educational context, but also the needs of those who will, in large measure, determine the success or failure of the enterprise.

Social Transition
American society is experiencing radical change. Peter Drucker, in *The Age of Discontinuity* (1969), observed that contemporary society has broken with the traditions of the past. Now, more than ever, the meaning of his observations is becoming apparent. New technologies have created new industries

that have made existing industries obsolete, and future technologies are being developed from emerging knowledge. Major worldwide economic changes are occurring, and, most important, access to knowledge has become the crucial resource of modern economies. This access is determining industrial success and changing the character of work, the labor force, and education (Drucker in Harmon 1979, p. 2). Many futurists predict a transindustrial society will emerge that will focus on human growth and development rather than on economic and material growth (Harmon 1979; Ferguson 1980).

The changes occurring across the social and cultural fabric of the nation are forcing institutions and individuals alike to redefine both their roles and their contributions. Higher education is not exempt from this massive transition (see, for example, Furniss 1981, pp. 5–6). After many years of nurturing and support, higher education is being held accountable (Mortimer and McConnell 1978, pp. 267–68). Like the automotive and steel industries, higher education has begun to confront economic difficulties (Nichols 1982).

Transition in Education
Early evidence indicates that it is proving difficult for higher education to embrace the social, political, economic, and technological change that Drucker described. As he predicted, new highly specialized educational alternatives are developing and challenging the traditional role of higher education. Credentialized educational programs are now offered through business and industry such as the Wang Institute in the high technology arena, the Arthur D. Little program in the managerial arena, and the Massachusetts General Hospital programs in the health arena. Many more alternative institutes and training programs are emerging annually, challenging the traditional role of higher education in the preparation of qualified professional personnel. Of the 64 million adults involved in some form of training or education, fewer than 20 percent are in college (Guzzetta 1982, p. 11). Concurrently, new highly specialized technological alternatives are developing to increase access to knowledge. Access to computerized information networks is increasing at a phenomenal rate. Simultaneously, personal computers are becoming increasingly sophisticated and cost effective. Cable television, also, is emerging as a potential competitor in the marketplace. It is clear that these emergent technological

alternatives are increasing the accessibility of knowledge beyond the confines of the campus.

However, in addition to the technological onslaught, higher education is being confronted with an even greater threat than most contemporary industries: the nation's commitment to higher education is slackening. Evidence of the decline in education as a national priority can be garnered not only through the controversy surrounding the establishment of the Department of Education, but also through a review of monies allocated to the pursuit of higher education. Mortimer and McConnell (1978, pp. 2–3) indicate that postsecondary education not only has lost its favored status in the competition for public monies, but it is also subject to increasing governmental influence (see also Furniss 1981, pp. 5–28; Shulman 1979, p. 4). In the sixties the national issue was discrimination, and the government funded programs for specialized populations that changed the complexion of higher education. Now the national issue is employability, and the government is funding specialized technical training programs that are altering the breadth of higher education. It is becoming clear that federal interventions not only have altered the clientele of higher education, they also have altered the traditional academic balance of colleges and universities across the country.

As traditional support systems for higher education change, colleges and universities are finding it increasingly difficult to maintain accessibility and deliver educational quality. Anticipating a decline in student aid, President Botstein of Bard College has expressed concern for the disparity between educational cost and educational choice: "We're in danger of having the better private institutions become an upper-class system" (Levey 1982). Given the increased emphasis on jobs, President Gander of Marlboro College has expressed concern for the devaluation of the liberal arts: "It looks as though we're hell-bent on becoming a nation of data processors" (Levey 1982). And, acknowledging both the tension created by decreasing access and increasing employability, President Giamatti of Yale University is concerned with the quality of the educational enterprise in light of the compromises being made by institutions and teachers alike:

There are thousands of people out there with Ph.D.s who can't go to work. We have these academic gypsies in this country—Bedouin tribes in vans. Places pick them up part time and they move on. There's a tremendous proletariat of Ph.D.s who are being used as migrant labor and their institutional loyalty is nil, because no institution has ever been loyal to them or paid them anything. And yet they hang on because they're good hardworking folk and they want to teach. But it has created a disaffected, embittered class within the academic world that sooner or later will bite back (Levey 1982).

Professional Transition

The transitions and stresses of the age of discontinuity have profoundly affected the profession, the institutions, and the faculty. Our colleges and universities have been educating massive, diverse student populations despite the students' lack of preparation and narrow concentration on specific vocational objectives. As revenues fail to keep pace with inflation, the educational enterprise has experienced chronic poverty. Yet, students have been educated, research has continued, and the public has been served through struggle and ingenuity. To a large extent, however, Minter and Bowen (1982, p. 7) also indicate that these achievements have come "out of the hides of faculty members." With recent increases in the numbers of part-time faculty, the faculty ranks have been growing slightly, but the ratio of full-time faculty to students has declined. At the same time, the percentage of faculty leaving education also has declined, but the percentage of faculty on tenure has increased slowly. Faculty salaries also have increased, but the economic position of faculty actually has deteriorated further (American Council on Education 1982, p. 3). Public institutions have increased teaching loads substantially and have reduced such amenities as secretarial assistance, research support, and professional travel (Minter and Bowen 1982, p. 8). As a result of these changes, faculty are receiving less support but have increased responsibility.

The balance in our colleges and universities is shifting away from teaching and toward managerial efficiency. Gene Maeroff notes that "schools, in adjusting to fiscal realities, may soon have more in common with business and industry than many educators thought possible" (Maeroff 1982, p. A15). By implementing business management techniques, colleges and universities may operate more efficiently, but it is doubtful that instruction will become more effective. Faculty have experienced a continued loss of economic and social status both

Faculty are receiving less support but have increased responsibility.

Developing Faculty Careers

within and beyond the campus. They are also confronted with decreased mobility, fewer rewards, declining resources, and increased student and collegial responsibility. As a result of these accumulated losses, faculty commitment to the institution can be expected to dwindle. As the struggle for survival intensifies, the disparity between the goals of the institution and the goals of the faculty is increasing. Further demands will increase the depersonalization and alienation of faculty if their needs are not taken into account.

ADULT AND CAREER DEVELOPMENT

Adult Development

In the past 20 years, interest in adult development has mushroomed. Although the study of adulthood was initiated by Freud and Jung, Erik Erikson's early work (1950) represented the first systematic attempt to chart the stages of normal, predictable human development. To this day, his work provides the framework for many studies of human growth and change.

Erikson (1950) described eight developmental stages between infancy and old age and identified the major developmental task that must be addressed at each stage (see table 1). As individuals age, they confront each developmental task directly, revising and reviewing all subsequent stages in relation to the dominant conflict. For this reason, Erikson maintains that it is essential to remain aware of the struggles of the earlier, formative stages when considering the issues to be confronted in adulthood.

Throughout the earliest stages, the individual develops a sense of hope, will, purpose, and competence. Through adolescence and early adulthood, the individual develops a sense of fidelity and love. During adulthood and old age, the longest of the developmental periods, the individual develops a sense of caring and of wisdom (Erikson and Erikson 1981, p. 251).

By showing what academics can expect to experience as they grow older, adult development theory helps provide a better understanding of predictable faculty needs. Similarly, career development theory can help demythologize the academic profession and can provide new perspectives on the problems inherent in contemporary faculty careers.

Levinson (1978), building on the work of Erikson, focuses more specifically on adulthood and describes three major periods: early adulthood, ages 17 to 45; middle adulthood, ages 40 to 65; and late adulthood, ages 60 to death (See table 2). As described by Levinson, each stage is defined and coupled to the next through an overlapping transitional period.

For Levinson (1978), early adulthood is characterized by a powerful connection between personal drives and societal requirements. At some points these connections reinforce one another, and at other points they contradict one another. Middle adulthood introduces a period of individuation that allows for the possibility of continued self-renewal and creative involvement. At this stage, individuals achieve new levels of meaning, awareness, and understanding, which prompt the emergence of a more defined individual and a more balanced life. During late

TABLE 1
ERIKSON'S EIGHT DEVELOPMENTAL STAGES

							Integrity vs. Despair	Old Age
						Generativity vs. Self-Absorption		Adulthood
					Intimacy vs. Isolation			Young Adulthood
				Identity vs. Confusion				Adolescence
			Industry vs. Inferiority					School Age
		Initiative vs. Guilt						Play Age
	Autonomy vs. Shame/Doubt							Early Childhood
Trust vs. Mistrust								Infancy

Adapted from: Erik H. Erikson, *Childhood and Society* (1950), p. 234.

TABLE 2
LEVINSON'S DEVELOPMENTAL STAGES

CHILDHOOD & ADOLESCENCE

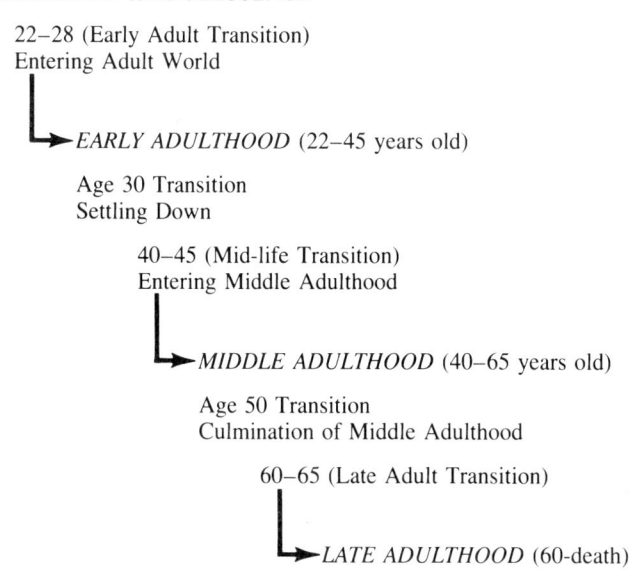

22–28 (Early Adult Transition)
Entering Adult World

　→ *EARLY ADULTHOOD* (22–45 years old)

　　Age 30 Transition
　　Settling Down

　　　40–45 (Mid-life Transition)
　　　Entering Middle Adulthood

　　　　→ *MIDDLE ADULTHOOD* (40–65 years old)

　　　　　Age 50 Transition
　　　　　Culmination of Middle Adulthood

　　　　　　60–65 (Late Adult Transition)

　　　　　　　→ *LATE ADULTHOOD* (60-death)

Adapted from: Levinson, *The Seasons of a Man's Life* (1978), p. 57.

adulthood, individuals must establish a new balance between social and self-involvement. The development of a stronger sense of self at this time reduces interest in social rewards and increases interest in the use of inner resources. This appraisal results in a sense of integrity and effects a reconciliation with acknowledged imperfections.

In Erikson's view (1950, 1978), the key developmental crisis in adulthood occurs with the struggle for generativity. The task facing individuals during this period is to learn to respond to adult responsibilities productively. Those who are unable to advance into generativity often regress into stagnation and personal impoverishment. Following Erikson, many authors on adult development (Gould 1978; Levinson 1978; Sheehy 1977; Davitz and Davitz 1976) have paid particular attention to this stage, sometimes referring to it as "the mid-life crisis." Gould (1978) and Levinson (1978) each describe a period of upheaval and turmoil at this time during which major changes occur in both personal lives and careers. For some individuals, a single culminating event may initiate a reappraisal of a subsequent mid-life transition. Sheehy (1977) describes the development of a sense of well-being that is derived from a sustained attitude of equanimity.

Moving beyond the experiences of adulthood, Erikson's current inquiries (1981) explore two themes. The first theme is that of diversity or the need to provide for alternatives; the second theme is that of community or the need for peer association. Erikson suggests that developing alternatives to be explored together with a sense of community enables adults to achieve integrity as they approach old age and to avoid its contrary, despair.

Common to each of these explorations of adult development is the conviction that individuals grow and change throughout their lives; that they move through a series of predictable stages; and that each stage presents a specific task or challenge and may provoke a crisis. Depending on the success with which individuals negotiate the challenges, they can achieve a sense of individuality, integrity, and personal well-being. Although the contributions of the individual may change over time, those who are successful in facing the challenges of their own individual development are most likely to contribute meaningfully to society throughout their lives.

Career Development
The continuing exploration of adult developmental stages has been paralleled by a growing interest in the way careers change. Most life cycle theorists perceive the development of an individual's career as central to the exploration of social norms and individual identity. Erikson (1950) describes the development of a sense of personal competence; Levinson (1978) and Gould (1978) describe the establishment of a "successful" professional identity in early adulthood followed by a revitalization of this identity in middle adulthood; Sheehy (1981) describes the development of a sense of purpose. In attempting to describe the impact of occupational status on the development of a sense of well-being, Sheehy indicates that self-respect appears to have a greater positive impact on satisfaction than does material wealth. She indicates that successful, well-educated professionals and the self-employed express a higher degree of satisfaction with their lives than do blue-collar workers (Sheehy 1981, p. 19). Perhaps this phenomenon can be explained by the fact that job security or a good salary is no longer sufficient

reward for work. Increasingly, individuals want a psychic return for their labors—satisfaction (Harmon 1979, p. 52).

Hall (1976, p. 53) describes five stages of career development that are compatible with the developmental tasks of the life cycle: growth, exploration, establishment, maintenance, and decline (see table 3). Each of these career development stages parallels the tasks encountered in the stages of individual development elaborated by Erikson.

TABLE 3
SUMMARY OF CAREER STAGE MODELS

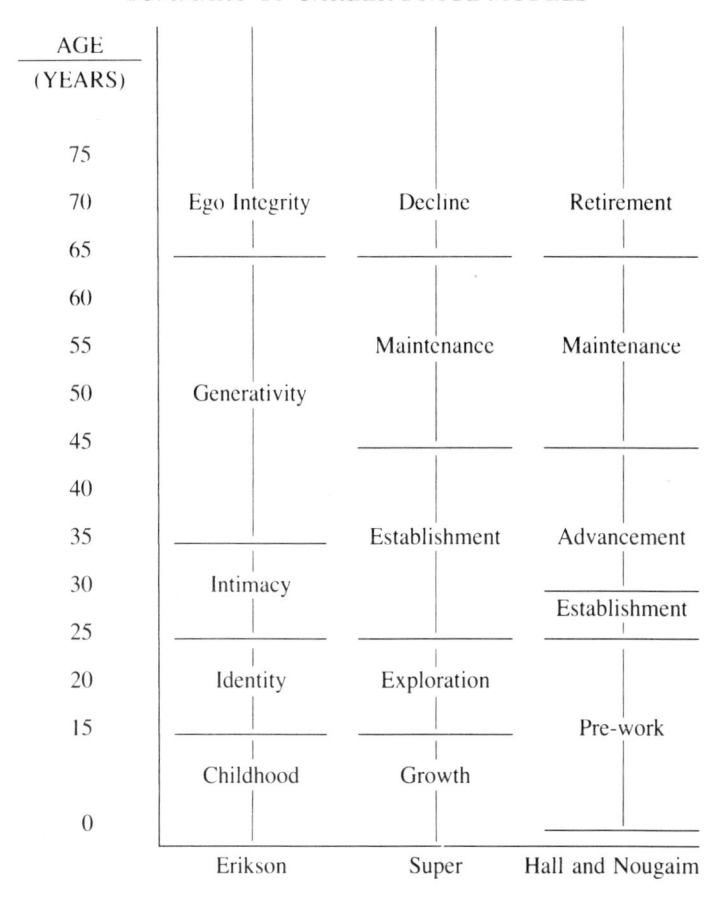

AGE (YEARS)	Erikson	Super	Hall and Nougaim
75			
70	Ego Integrity	Decline	Retirement
65			
60			
55		Maintenance	Maintenance
50	Generativity		
45			
40			
35		Establishment	Advancement
30	Intimacy		
25			Establishment
20	Identity	Exploration	
15			Pre-work
	Childhood	Growth	
0			

Adapted from: Hall, *Careers in Organizations* (1976), p. 56.

During the establishment stage, the task is that of locating work compatible with the values and goals of the individual.

Developing Faculty Careers

Between the ages of 25 and 45, the objectives are establishment and advancement in the field chosen. By middle adulthood, white-collar careers usually are reaching the end of the establishment stages and are beginning the maintenance stage. Just as the generativity stage is critical to the future of the individual, the maintenance stage can be critical to the future of the career. Some individuals continue to grow in mid-career; others begin to decline. Finally, as cues are received indicating that the limit of advancement has been reached, the need to compete decreases. This reduction in competitive drive often results in reduced productivity and career commitment.

The literature on career development, like the literature on adult development, indicates that careers are no longer viewed as static. Rather they, like individuals, are seen as changing. Juxtaposing the two sets of theories, the relationship between career and adult development is dynamic: changes in individuals affect their careers and vice versa. This dynamism results in changing substantive contributions to the workplace on the part of the individual. It also results in changing attachments to the career. For, although every individual has the potential to continue to grow and develop throughout life, it appears that all careers reach a plateau and, eventually, go into decline. This realization suggests that employers need to be aware that, beyond a certain point, the needs of the individual will almost certainly take precedence over the needs of the career, and, therefore, the organization.

FACULTY CAREERS

Beyond the general theory of career development stages lie the specific demands and challenges of an academic career. To understand the kinds of challenges faculty members face requires an awareness of the singular characteristics that differentiate an academic career from other professional careers. First among those characteristics is the lack of professional identity among academics (Freedman et al. 1979, p. 2). This lack may in part be attributable to the fact that no single element of the work academics do sets them apart from all other professionals. In *Reshaping Faculty Careers*, W. Todd Furniss says:

> *They [academics] are not the only ones who teach, or who teach college-age students, or who teach physics, or who do research on economic depressions and recessions. Nor are they the only ones who are organized into departments dealing with a single area of study or interest, or even the only professionals employed by a college or university. Their identity as faculty members is a loose combination of these and other factors (Furniss 1981, p. 41).*

A second remarkable characteristic of an academic career is that although most academics spend most of their time teaching (Ladd 1979), very few originally set their sights on teaching as a career goal (Light, Marsden, and Carl 1973, p. 16). What aspiring academics choose is an area of specialization for graduate school: teaching tends to be a more or less inevitable consequence or by-product of staying in the academic world. As a result, faculty by and large drift into their role as teachers rather than actively choosing that role (Baldwin et al. 1981, p. 81). Here too, the difference between academe and other learned professions is pronounced: one hardly drifts into the practice of medicine, law, or divinity. People who left other careers to enter academe are an important exception to this general observation. For them, and they make up almost 25 percent of higher education faculty, teaching represents a clear career choice (Light, Marsden, and Carl 1973, p. 51). They wanted to teach and often hold a very different view of the demands and rewards of teaching from the view held by those who never left the academic milieu but moved steadily from college to graduate school to doctoral studies (with a teaching assistantship) and eventually into a full-time faculty position.

Third, the preparation graduate students receive bears little resemblance to what they do when they become faculty

The preparation graduate students receive bears little resemblance to what they do when they become faculty members.

Developing Faculty Careers

members. During the years of graduate study, teaching typically receives little attention. The focus and emphasis in graduate school are on the chosen discipline or specialization. This same scale of values carries over into the attitude of many full-time faculty. When academics talk shop they almost never discuss their teaching, and this has been cited as "perhaps the clearest evidence that teaching undergraduates is not a true profession" (Freedman et al. 1979, p. 8).

The Faculty Role
The direct, on-the-job experience of faculty heightens and intensifies the dichotomy between what they have prepared to do and what they are expected to do. At every level in higher education, teaching conflicts with graduate training and research (Light, Marsden, and Carl 1973, p. 3). Making matters even more difficult is an academic reward structure that so heavily favors research that teaching effectiveness is practically irrelevant to professional advancement (Tuckman 1979). Thus, faculty find themselves caught between two unconnected sets of demands. Most think of themselves as teachers, not as scholars; most give little, if any, time to research (Ladd 1979; Shulman 1979); and virtually *all* are expected to do substantial amounts of teaching. But, if they are interested in getting ahead, faculty must satisfy criteria far removed from their everyday duties and responsibilities.

More than any other factor, this unresolved discordance between traditional graduate training and the task of teaching and between the task of teaching and the academic reward system hinders the development of a clear professional identity for faculty.

The new faculty member quickly discovers other characteristics of an academic career. An academic career is a solitary career and teaching is a solitary activity. Faculty tend to be left very much to their own devices; they receive little guidance and few opportunities to discuss problems (see Bess 1977, p. 250). There is a common perception that the faculty member is monarch in his or her classroom. Intermittent, one-shot observations do little to replace that perception with a sense of teaching as a shared enterprise based on a common pool of skills and practices known to be effective.

Moreover, not only are support and reinforcement almost nonexistent, but the enormously demanding task of teaching well yields few internal rewards. Indeed, few faculty can articulate their own criteria for deciding whether a course they are teaching is going well or can offer any rationale for what they do in the classroom. But,

without means to evaluate one's teaching . . . the professor is denied the most elementary satisfaction—seeing desirable things happen as a result of planned action (Freedman et al. 1979, p. 8).

When faculty are asked to describe the role of the teacher, it becomes clear that they are not a homogeneous group. They express qualitatively different viewpoints in describing the demands of teaching. Geis and Smith (1981) suggest that faculty have difficulty conceptualizing and talking about teaching. Although some discuss teaching with reference to students, most faculty agree that teaching is extremely personal and that it is closely identified with the teacher. Moreover, the results of the labors of teaching are, for all intents and purposes, ineffable. As one faculty member put it, "You knock yourself out in a course, and the kids tell you you're a failure" (Davitz and Davitz 1976, p. 98). And, if the students tell faculty they've failed, in a sense they have to accept that verdict since there are no generally accepted standards for the measurement of teaching effectiveness.

Faculty soon catch on to the fundamentally unchanging nature of their work. With the exception of special projects, what a faculty member does one year is pretty much what he or she will do the next year and the year after and the year after. This lack of variety tends to cause teaching to become more and more enervating (Bess 1977, p. 249). Faculty members mature as the years go by: physically, psychologically, and in terms of their philosophy and technique. But the essential sameness of their lives remains. What many academics need, and academe rarely provides, is a chance to diversify, to change, even for a short while, their everyday routine (Baldwin et al. 1981, p. 3).

Thus, an academic career has a number of characteristics that make it especially demanding. They are: a poorly defined professional identity, a long period of preparation that focuses on research and ignores teaching, and a reward system that follows suit. Further complicating matters is the lack of consensus among academics about the art or craft of teaching. There is disagreement about whether pedagogy should be regarded as a valid discipline and education as an appropriate field for graduate study. Many academics feel that the quality of teaching cannot be measured (Light, Marsden, and Carl 1973, p. 57), and the involvement of students in the evaluation of teaching effectiveness is still a sensitive matter on which strong, opposing views are held.

Compounding these difficulties is the ambivalence of the faculty themselves about the real objective value of teaching. Although most faculty spend most of their time teaching and describe themselves as teachers, they place a higher value on research than they place on teaching. Scholarship and research are readily rewarded through the profession, the institution, and external sources; rewards for teaching excellence typically remain very weak (Ladd 1979, p. 5). Few faculty are engaged in publication and research, and yet these few are widely recognized for their achievements while outstanding teachers are not.

Faculty are entering the profession with stronger credentials in their disciplines than they were 20 years ago. The majority are actively engaged in teaching and carry a substantial course load of 9 to 12 hours a week (Grant and Lind 1978, p. 97). According to the Ladd-Lipset survey, they spend most of their workweek, averaging 44 hours, in teaching and preparation, with a median of 4 hours a week devoted to research and scholarly writing (Ladd 1979, p. 3). Less than one-fourth of the professoriate has published extensively, and more than half have published very little or nothing at all, particularly within the community college ranks. Faculty preferences corroborate these findings. Ladd reports that for every one professor devoted to research there are five others who are devoted to teaching and that

> *Most academics think of themselves as "teachers" and "professionals," not as "scholars," "scientists," or "intellectuals"—and they perform accordingly (Ladd 1979, pp. 1, 4).*

Faculty Career Stages

Frequently, junior faculty, having received encouragement from a mentor, enter the profession with high expectations. Hodgkinson (1974) indicates that they may dream of making scholarly contributions or pursuing large research projects (Hodgkinson 1974, p. 266). Ladd, likewise, indicates that the younger faculty are more likely to have significant interests in research (Ladd 1979, p. 4). These faculty, who traverse from college directly into teaching, probably have already experienced a rather high degree of isolation from the psychological, economic, and social demands of others as they enter the job market. In fact, Hodgkinson (1974, p. 265) believes that most of them "are divorced from the world of manual labor and know very little about careers and skills outside higher education."

As young faculty members begin to grow in the role, they, like other professionals, encounter a transitional period at about age 30. Over the decade that follows, these faculty begin to try to locate themselves within the organization and strive to achieve a position of some autonomy and importance (Hodgkinson 1974, p. 268). After a period of dependence prompted by education's notoriously slow reward system, the faculty begin to establish themselves as individuals by achieving tenure and committee assignments or by publishing and conducting research. Ultimately, they begin to shed the illusions of their earlier dreams and expectations, revising, but not eliminating, their essence.

As the next decade, and mid-life crisis, approaches, Hodgkinson indicates that the faculty begin to question the viability of their chosen profession, particularly in comparison with others such as the legal or medical professions (Hodgkinson 1974, p. 270). They reassess the status of the institution, their status among their peers, and their own sense of automony, influence, and power. They also consider their prospects. As Hodgkinson notes, "from the perspective of a full professor, age 40, with tenure, the reward structure for the next 25 years before retirement . . . is fairly grim . . ." (Hodgkinson 1974, p. 270). Again, the dream is revisited and revised; some stay in education, and others, recognizing their last chance to reestablish themselves, leave.

For those who survive their thirties and forties, there emerges a new loyalty to the institution because they have accepted it "for what it is," not for what it might have become. Many faculty find meaningful alternatives to supplement teaching and research during this period, and almost all faculty begin to define their own goals and levels of productivity. At the same time, however, they also become aware of their own limitations—limitations of energy, time, and stamina.

Within a few years of retirement, faculty begin to realize that they have passed their peak. They also begin to realize that they have few options. Some "tough it out"; others simply "hang on." Still others seem to decline very little, and a few "reach the heights of their powers" (Hodgkinson 1974, p. 273).

Implicit in a review of faculty careers are the assumptions that faculty, like other workers, go through predictable career stages, and that they, like others, reduce their level of professional involvement and commitment as they advance in their careers. Baldwin (1979) has attempted to synthesize the stage-related theories of faculty careers in higher education, relating them to the stage-related theories of adult and career development.

Baldwin (1979), like Hodgkinson (1974), associates the early years of college teaching with Levinson's (1978) characterization of early adulthood during which the occupation and the dream are established.

Furniss (1981) sees Levinson's (1978) formulation as dividing a male faculty member's career into three principal seasons. As a young adult, the faculty member enters academia, and, with the support of a mentor, moves toward getting tenure and settling down in his career. This stage, or season, ends at about the age of 40 when there is a mid-life transitional period of up to five years. Following the mid-life transition the faculty member moves into middle adulthood. The next 10 years (approximately) see the faculty member developing his autonomy, taking on the role of mentor, and broadening his range of interests beyond his own discipline and classes. The third season, late adulthood, beginning in the mid-fifties after another period of transition, brings a reduction in competitiveness, more interests outside the campus, and a move into the role of elder statesman (Furniss 1981, p. 84).

Given the isolation common to the profession, attempts have been made to integrate the growth of the individual in the role of the faculty. Ralph (1978), convinced that an understanding of personality development is key to professional adaptation, defined five distinct stages of personality development of faculty in higher education (see table 4). These five stages move along a continuum from a highly moralistic view of personality to what is called a psychologically insightful view of personality.

In the first stage the goals and roles of new faculty are defined in accord with the peer group. Generally, these goals focus on form rather than content, and the role of the teacher is characterized in rather simplistic terms as that of pouring knowledge into the vessel. New faculty, therefore, might be

TABLE 4
RALPH'S CONCEPTION OF THE DEVELOPMENT OF FACULTY

STAGE	CHARACTERISTICS	
ONE	Reference group defines role and goals; knowledge viewed in absolute terms to be assimilated by students.	MORALISTIC VIEW
TWO	Distance increases from reference group; views of knowledge and education become more complex.	
THREE	Awareness of alternatives in teaching increases as does uncertainty on integration of available choices; knowledge is viewed in problematic terms, and education occurs in a conducive environment with active effort.	
FOUR	Role conflicts are mastered, and a personal style evolves with a sense of reciprocity; students must synthesize diverse facts, explore complexity, and discover answers.	PSYCHOLOGICALLY INSIGHTFUL VIEW
FIVE	Acceptance of contradiction, ambivalence, diversity, and complexity results in a clearly articulated educational philosophy; appreciation of the student situation and style evolves, and satisfaction with student relationships develops.	

Adapted from: Ralph, "Faculty Development: A Stage Conception" (1978), p. 62.

expected to provide extremely teacher-centered instruction using an approach such as lecturing.

At the second stage, faculty continue to define their role in relationship to the reference group but begin to establish increasing distance. At the same time, their view of knowledge increases in complexity, and the role is defined through the provision of facts and assistance. During this stage, for example, the highly teacher-centered lecture format may be buttressed with increasing tutorial support.

At stage three, faculty develop an awareness of the possible alternatives in teaching but remain uncertain as to the integration of the available choices. Faculty at this stage begin to define their role as that of creating conditions in which students learn through active participation. During this stage, the faculty

Developing Faculty Careers

may experiment and expand their teaching repertoire using systematized instructional formats that promote student-teacher participation.

By the fourth stage, faculty have evolved a sense of freedom and relativity in social roles with a compatible style of functioning. They have begun to develop a sense of reciprocity in their role through which students must synthesize information and discover answers for themselves. During the fourth stage, the faculty may develop increasingly more student-centered instruction that promotes student involvement in the learning process.

At the last stage, faculty can articulate an educational philosophy that includes a sense of values and character. They appreciate the students' situation and find satisfaction in relationships with them. At this final stage, the teacher accepts diversity, contradiction, ambivalence, and irony while continuing to perform effectively. The teaching repertoire includes a high degree of discussion and orchestrated digression.

Outcomes

Brookes (1980) has identified three psychological outcomes of a faculty career. Some faculty exhibit the characteristics of generativity adumbrated by Erikson; others, having apparently been unsuccessful in the struggle for generativity, show signs of self-absorption and stuckness. Most, however, fall between the two end points of the continuum from generativity to self-absorption. These "insulated" faculty express a high level of job satisfaction, are well-versed in their discipline, and are perceived as effective in the classroom. Unlike generative faculty, insulated academics see teaching as a job, not a calling. They are thorough and conscientious, but give no more to the institution than is required. They have little involvement in committee structures, extracurricular activities, and curriculum development. Many faculty in this category have modified the institution to suit their own personal needs, particularly with regard to their teaching schedules and assignments. Still, they do not describe the adversarial relationships frequently articulated by stuck faculty. The role of the individual institution in this slow withdrawal from active involvement remains unclear. It may be that certain characteristics of an academic career, particularly the unchanging nature of the task, the absence of external standards for success, and the abbreviated career ladders contribute to the withdrawal process. It may be that the environment is more conducive to continued growth on some campuses than it is on others.

Sudano (1982) gives a light-hearted but insightful portrait of the stages of this withdrawal process.

After the fifth year: You begin to regard student evaluations of your teaching with less terror and more humor. After the tenth year: You stop assigning 10–15 page papers. . . . You give up writing new course proposals. You keep your mouth shut during faculty meetings. After the fifteenth year: You figure out a way to get out of attending graduation ceremonies. After the twentieth year: You get really interested in your retirement program. . . . You keep your smile to yourself when bright young instructors come up with "new". . . ideas.

In general, the culture of higher education is not particularly conducive to the development of the individual faculty member (Freedman et al. 1979). Teaching remains a solitary activity, education remains an isolated profession, and academe offers little career guidance or support for faculty. Institutions attempt to create homogeneity across faculty ranks and the norms of the profession inhibit faculty members' attempts to satisfy their needs for affiliation and community. Even in research, faculty are reticent to share problems and pleasures (Bess 1977, p. 250). Furthermore, the academic culture is not tolerant. Teaching often is perceived as a "one life—one career" profession; those who leave are considered to be, in some sense, ineffective (quoted in Furniss 1981, pp. 1–2). A move from teaching into academic administration is tolerated rather than encouraged. A common tenet in academia is still "once a faculty member always a faculty member." The corollary, that the academic workplace provides everything a reasonable faculty member could want, is rapidly losing popularity and credibility.

At each stage of their academic careers, faculty face a complex matrix of growing and changing needs and aspirations. As maturing adults, they experience personal challenges and face psychosocial tasks. Each of these tasks offers the possibility for further growth and progress toward generativity but also holds the danger of a regression towards stagnation and self-absorption (Erikson and Erikson 1958). As academics, faculty continuously develop, revise, and reestablish their professional goals

. . . the culture of higher education is not particularly conducive to the development of the individual faculty member.

Developing Faculty Careers 25

and aspirations. As teachers, they expand their perceptions of students, their awareness of the potential of learning, and their ability to engage the dynamism of teaching. The trouble is that current pressures in higher education are forcing faculty at all stages of their careers into uncongenial and ungenerative roles. As Furniss says:

> *For the older faculty member, there may seem no longer to be a suitable role. Yeats said it: "That is no country for old men." On the one hand, he (or she) is too expensive and should be moved out as quickly as bribes or the law will allow. Part of the push will be assignments to work suitable for the entrepreneurial, middle-adult faculty member or even for the ungrown youth, but not for older persons. For the mid-season faculty member, a time of exploration is denied ("no funds") or narrowed to repetitions of courses or an overburden of the unexciting students who show up everywhere. For the young, the competition is now not only with peers . . . but also with the middle-aged and older faculty (Furniss 1981, p. 85).*

DEVELOPING SOLUTIONS

So far the academic world barely has begun to come to grips with these complex issues. Some attempts to tackle them have been made through faculty development programs. However, the role of faculty development has undergone a number of major changes as the demands placed on higher education have changed.

Although the term "faculty development" is a comparative newcomer to the jargon of higher education, by 1978 more than half the accredited colleges in the country had established programs and practices for faculty renewal and the improvement of instruction (Stordahl 1981). This widespread institutional acceptance of formal programs to promote faculty development was accompanied by profound changes in attitudes toward faculty members' growth and in the kinds of opportunities for self-renewal available to faculty.

Changing Role of Faculty Development

Before the rise of faculty development programs, the tradition of higher education was to encourage and support the development of faculty through sabbaticals and other leaves, research grants and special projects, visiting lectureships, released time, colloquia, exchanges, and conference participation. This tradition is characterized by its emphasis on scholarly endeavors and by the initiating role assumed by faculty. The role of the institution was supportive, providing faculty with the time or the resources they needed to pursue their own scholarly interests. Although the motivation for such support may not have been purely altruistic, the interests of the institution in this process were clearly subordinate to those of the individual. For the most part, colleges and universities were content to accept as their reward the reflected glory of the scholars whose work brought them prestige, funding, and students.

The first of a series of changes in the role of faculty development can be traced to the demands of the Sputnik Era. At that time the federal government, particularly through the National Science Foundation, extended the role it had assumed during World War II and offered large grants for scientific and technological research that supported national priorities. Academics responded by expanding programs in engineering, mathematics, and the laboratory sciences. They also developed innovative curricula, such as the new math, and accelerated conceptually based approaches in physics and chemistry. The goal of these projects was to equip students with the skills and

Developing Faculty Careers

knowledge needed in order to accept the many challenges implicit in this country's determination to beat the Russians to the moon.

Other changes came with the social revolution of the sixties when many academic traditions were questioned and, over time, changed. Growing social awareness and increased federal support made higher education accessible to massive new populations who crowded campuses previously enlarged to accommodate World War II veterans. Following the law of supply and demand, colleges expanded programs, services, personnel, and facilities to meet the newly created needs.

By the end of the sixties, these new students were questioning the relevance of the traditional curriculum. Significant increases in educational opportunities for disadvantaged students and for adult learners, bilingual students, handicapped students, and other nontraditional students brought pressure on faculty to change the focus of college curricula from the needs of the discipline to the needs of the students. The validity of core and distribution requirements was hotly debated; traditional grading systems frequently were replaced by nonpunitive ways of evaluating students' progress. In addition, the draft status of young men during the war in Vietnam subjected many faculty and many institutions to increased moral and ethical pressures. These pressures often spilled over into what previously had been seen as purely academic matters.

The resulting shifts in educational purpose and philosophy caused lasting changes in the academic community. It was acknowledged that students learn in many ways and at differing rates, depending on their preparation. Academic advising recognized the importance and validity of students' personal and career goals and attempted to integrate these with academic goals. To a limited extent, students were accepted as consumers, and the college became a marketplace.

Faculty Development Programs
The response to this second onslaught was a rapid acceleration of efforts intended to help faculty adapt to new students and new circumstances. Because the sixties and early seventies were a time of affluence, the federal government, foundations, corporations, and colleges and universities were able to provide substantial financial support for all kinds of faculty development. Faculty development became an identifiable educational industry complete with curriculum, instructional specialists and

consultants, a literature, advocate, and critics. Many campuses established an office of faculty development and year-round development programs. By 1973, the American Association of Community and Junior Colleges (AACJC) had allied itself to the faculty development movement. In its annual report, the association urged the acceptance of staff development as a first rank priority (in Hammons 1975, p. xi). In 1976 Centra did a major survey of faculty development identifying 45 different faculty development practices ranging from sabbatical leaves to awards for teaching excellence. By 1978 a majority of accredited institutions of higher education had some kind of formal program of faculty development (Stordahl 1981). In 1979 ERIC contained more than 18,500 items on staff development (Brookes 1980, p. 25) that provided massive documentation of the concepts and language of faculty development programs.

But although faculty development programs multiplied, basic questions about their focus and purpose often went unanswered. Some development programs focused on faculty members, some on the courses taught by faculty, some on the teaching/learning environment (Gaff 1975, p. 63). There was concern at what appeared to be a conflict between personal development and professional development (Freedman et al. 1979, p. 4). Gaff (1975) described development programs focused on the organization, the instruction, and the faculty. Berquist and Phillips (1975) described development programs focused on the organization, the instruction, and the person. Toombs (1975) focused on programmatic planning that integrated institutional, curricular, and professional levels of development into a three-dimensional model, and Ralph (1978) described faculty development programming that addressed the teacher directly in an effort to enhance the teacher's ability to help students develop themselves. In 1980 Wurster and McCartney articulated the outcome of faculty development: "The ultimate end [sic] of faculty development is to improve the quality of education, to reemphasize the basic teaching mission of the institution" (Wurster and McCartney 1980, p. 15).

Ultimately, faculty development was distinguished from organizational or institutional development, professional development, and staff development. Yet, the single biggest difference between these development programs and traditional growth opportunities for faculty was that the new programs were not research-centered. They advocated innovations in curriculum design and instructional techniques rather than supporting the eclectic scholarly endeavors of individual faculty. Moreover, their acknowledged goal was the "improvement" of faculty, a goal that left the impression that faculty did not possess the knowledge or skills required for the work they had been hired to do. Given the scant attention paid to pedagogy in most graduate programs, it can be argued that most faculty could benefit from assistance in improving the design of their courses and in increasing the range of their teaching techniques. But this push to "improve" faculty ignored the basic division in academe between teaching and research and did not allow for the fact that in higher education it is research that is rewarded, not teaching.

Perhaps the greatest change in faculty development was the shift in focus from support of individual scholarly endeavors to attempts to deal with concerns. Certainly many fundamental questions about faculty development programs went unanswered. These unanswered questions include how to divide responsibility for the programs between the faculty and the institution, whether the institution should sponsor such programs (Furniss 1981, pp. 130–32), and whether the goal of faculty development should be *teacher* improvement or *teaching* improvement (Bess 1977, p. 255). Most seriously, the new approaches to faculty development, unlike the traditional approach, rarely succeeded in being made a part of the formal academic reward structure. Hence, it is not surprising that neither the level of faculty participation nor the results achieved by faculty development programs were very impressive. A study completed in 1979 (Geis and Smith 1981) reported that only 25 percent of faculty made use of these formal faculty development programs, and that this percentage included a large number of repeaters. Moreover, many of the designs and techniques imparted by these programs fell short of providing solutions to the long-term problem of dealing effectively with the expectations and needs of the new students. One study reported that:

> *A recent review of faculty renewal efforts concludes that such projects have had little success, and that the result is not surprising. The reason suggested is that "so little is arranged in a way that affects the real life and interests of the faculty members" (Ferren and White 1977, p. 23).*

Presumably, some faculty gradually integrated new techniques into their teaching as a result of development programs, but it has become increasingly difficult to identify specific changes such programs were designed to induce. This difficulty is exacerbated by the fact that, as is common in most emerging efforts, evaluation was not a strong component of most faculty development programs. A review in 1978 observed that the effectiveness of faculty development practices "is not yet entirely known" (Centra 1978, p. 201). Had the word "entirely" been deleted, the comment would have lost little of its accuracy.

Faculty Career Development

By the late seventies the faculty development bandwagon had all but lumbered to a halt. Circumstances had changed once again. Higher education was battling for survival and, true to Maslow, had neither the time nor the resources to spend on expensive programs that yielded only nebulous results. Institutions had to find a way to adjust to an unfavorable economic climate, a steady decline in the traditional college-age population, little or no growth, an aging faculty, and a huge swing in student enrollments from the liberal arts to career and job-related disciplines.

In response to the new circumstances, faculty development went through a third major change. The focus shifted back to the individual faculty member, but the motivation for this shift was once again institutional rather than individual need. To cite a typical caveat, "Faculty development programs that emphasize individual growth . . . must have safeguards for insuring that institutional needs are also met" (Wurster and McCartney 1980, p. 19). Individual growth contracts, retraining programs aimed at liberal arts faculty, and attempts to make faculty more productive through such innovations as programmed learning are representative of the kinds of opportunities that began to be offered to faculty.

This emphasis on serving the needs of the institution continues to characterize what is now beginning to be called "faculty career development." Some of the new programs have as much emphasis on helping faculty leave academe as they have on helping them grow. To this extent, higher education is adopting a corporate model of human resource development. Outplacement projects conducted by professional associations, growth contracts, and the development of early retirement incentives are typical of this new approach. Baldwin (1982) provides a good overview of the approaches now being explored or implemented. Career planning activities are encouraged by the

Serving the needs of the institution continues to characterize what is now . . . called "faculty career development."

Council for the Advancement of Small Colleges and Associated Schools of the Pacific Northwest, by Gordon College in Massachusetts, and by the Pennsylvania State Colleges Educational Services Trust Fund (see Baldwin et al. 1981, pp. 10–19). Retraining projects for faculty are in use in the University of Wisconsin System, California State College at Long Beach, The College of Saint Scholastica in Minnesota, and Mary College in North Dakota (Baldwin et al. 1981, pp. 20–30). Comprehensive career services, some specifically designed to help faculty expand their career options, are found in small colleges, large private and public universities, and public consortia (Baldwin et al. 1981, p. 45).

Although these initiatives have merit and are responsible attempts to meet new challenges, they also cannot help but reinforce the concerns of those who question the long-term viability of the traditional academic career and who worry about what higher education will be like by the end of the century.

PREPARING FOR THE YEAR 2,000

The upheavals of the past decade have resulted in major changes in our academic institutions and in faculty careers.

The Status Quo

As colleges and universities scramble to stay alive, they are faced with two overwhelming concerns: to hold deficits down and to keep enrollments up. Many colleges often appear more interested in reducing the size and cost of their faculties than in maintaining a collegial environment in which faculty members can thrive. Nor is this surprising. As Shulman (1979, p. 7) points out: "Holding down faculty salaries is for colleges the most effective method of combating inflation." However, realizing that all institutions mold and condition their employees (Freedman et al. 1979, p. 16), the reduced ability to care for faculty members' needs will, over time, reduce the commitment of faculty and the level of their institutional involvement. Because a core of dedicated people is important for all organizations (Baker 1973, p. 121), such a reduction in involvement and commitment eventually will have an adverse effect on quality of institutions (Baldwin et al. 1981, p. 2).

The signs of this erosion are becoming apparent. Institutions are investing heavily in business management techniques to enable them to operate more efficiently (Maeroff 1982). Traditional personnel policies, such as tenure, are being abridged; salaries are not keeping pace with the economy, and the faculty collegial role is at issue. Today the faculty feel "less involved in the important decisions about running their institutions" (Magarrell 1982). They perceive a decline in innovation, a penchant for curricular change that is financially rather than educationally driven, and a decline in morale linked more to the erosion of shared governance than to salary. A recent Carnegie Foundation report on governance echoed those concerns and recommended a revitalization of the collegial role in campus decision making (Carnegie 1982).

As the decade unfolds, two additional facts certainly will affect academic careers. First, fewer faculty will achieve tenure. Many will be hired on nontenure tracks; others will be denied tenure because of the already high percentage of tenured faculty on many campuses. Second, the majority of faculty is now between 35 and 45 years old (Shulman 1979, pp. 20, 21). Given decreased mobility and rewards, it is likely that these faculty will remain in education at their institutions for another 20 to

30 years. Therefore, by and large, most colleges already have the faculty with whom they will enter the twenty-first century.

Such a realization lends new urgency to the need to invest in the academic reward system and to support academic careers.

The Dilemma of the Reward Structure

It is almost 20 years since Caplow and McGee wrote:

> *Perhaps the leading problem for the individual faculty member is the incongruity between his job assignment and the work which determines his success or failure (Quoted by Light, Marsden, and Carl 1973, p. 58).*

Given the current economic and educational climate, this unchanged state of affairs is resulting in increasing ambivalence about the professional identity and the primary mission of academics. To what extent is an academic career a teaching career? The same title of "professor" is given to the research scientist who does almost no formal classroom teaching and to the faculty member who does no formal research, just as the medical profession bestows the title of "doctor" equally upon researchers and practitioners. Unlike the medical reward structure, however, the academic reward structure discriminates against the practitioner.

Although there may be some exceptions, the general rule is that the only sure route to academic advancement is via publication (Light, Marsden, and Carl 1973; Tuckman 1979). The rewards given to faculty who have published a large number of articles swamp those given to faculty engaged in virtually any other activity (Tuckman 1979). At the same time, we know (Ladd 1979) that 80 percent of academics are not writing for publication. Thus, a higher value is placed on one aspect of the work of a minority of faculty than on the primary occupation of the majority. At high level institutions, teaching ability is, in fact, almost irrelevant to promotion (Light, Marsden, and Carl 1973, p. 3). Apart from publication, the other route to academic advancement is administration. Large salary increases accompany the move from the classroom to the administration building, especially for men. Consequently, although only 7 percent of males with up to five years in higher education are involved in administration, in the 21 to 25 year cohort more than 21 percent are in administrative posts (Tuckman 1979, p. 180).

Complicating the whole issue of rewards for academics is the reward structure's built-in bias toward younger faculty. Once a person achieves tenure and a full professorship—and up to now most faculty eventually have achieved both by their mid-forties (Light, Marsden, and Carl 1973, pp. 35, 36)—there are virtually no extrinsic rewards for an institution to offer.

Unless some way is found to recognize and reward teaching, faculty will experience ever more acutely the dissonance between their assigned responsibilities and what their departments and institutions value. The tenure system pays no heed to the stages of adult development and provides neither incentives nor substantial rewards for continued growth. Similarly, achieving the rank of full professor means that one has reached the top rung of the very short academic career ladder. The tenured full professor who wants to stay vital and involved, and who wants some degree of reward or recognition, is virtually forced to turn away from the classroom toward further publication, a career in a professional society, administration, or a second career such as consulting.

This dilemma can be resolved by modifying higher education's traditional reward system. It is time for publication to be recognized and accepted as a form of teaching rather than as the be-all and end-all of academic endeavors. It is time for the kind of teaching that engages faculty for the majority of their careers to be given parity with research in the academic reward system.

Teaching is primarily a craft: it can be developed, polished, and perfected over a lifetime. Thus, it can satisfy adult needs for growth and can offset the feeling that, professionally, life ends with a tenured full professorship. Moreover, recognizing that teaching and research are complementary in higher education and have equal worth and importance would help develop a sense of community and support for diversity within academe.

In his most recent work, Erik Erikson (1981) has said that psychosocial well-being depends on the two elements of community and diversity. *Community* is the sense of belonging and of being part of a shared enterprise with common values and goals. *Diversity* encourages individuals to continue to grow and explore by providing a variety of opportunities and challenges. Hall and Nougaim's work also suggests that the need for affiliation (community) and self-actualization (diversity) increases as professionals advance in their careers. Institutions, preoccupied with their own self-preservation, are unlikely to take the initiative in dealing with these issues.

The Impact of Technology

Quite apart from the human need, there is another motive for initiating a drive to reestablish a true academic community supportive of individual diversity. The changes higher education has experienced in the last decade will be dwarfed by the changes sure to occur before the year 2,000. Extraordinary technological developments have vastly increased our ability to store, transmit, and gain access to huge quantities of information. Word processing; data processing; and electronic data storage, retrieval, and transfer are routine operations for ever-increasing numbers of people. Such developments undermine the assumption of the Carnegie Council's *3,000 Futures* (1980) that the next 20 years can be tackled pretty much as business-as-usual. As more and more students come to higher education familiar with the tools provided by technology, courses, colleges, and faculty will have to change and adapt.

It is impossible to predict the directions higher education will take. Distance learning, already taking place in many countries (Knapper 1982, pp. 5–22), will make it possible, for the first time, to reduce the faculty member's need to be a part of an established institution of higher education. The same technology also means that students will not have to attend college—literally and physically. Higher education—*formal* higher education—really could take place at home (Knapper 1982, p. 82).

The imponderable question is how academe will respond to these challenges and opportunities. Faculty tend to resist far-reaching change. They usually exhibit considerable resistance to "unorthodox" teaching methods and to nontraditional ways of earning credit. On some campuses, despite years of work by the Council for the Advancement of Experiential Learning, even the idea of granting credit for life experience or prior learning still is seen as radical and probably heretical. Many departments and many faculty have genuine difficulty in accepting that courses given on other campuses or in other departments are equal in quality to their own.

Hence, it is impossible to guess what use higher education will make of the opportunities the new technology presents. The value of a better mousetrap is apparent only to the person interested in catching mice. It is not clear how much interest most faculty have in getting education out of "their" classrooms and off "their" campuses. A few small-scale experimental operations, such as courses by newspaper or by television, are tolerated, but there is little evidence of widespread interest in expanding them.

Whatever changes come upon academe between now and the end of the century—and there are sure to be changes—it is certain that there will continue to be students in need of instruction. The challenge for higher education is first, to acknowledge that many different kinds of exchange take place between students and faculty; second, to find ways to evaluate effective teaching; and third, to reward those who teach well. By giving the art and craft of teaching the attention it merits, colleges and universities will be able to offer faculty two alternative career routes, research and teaching. In this way, institutions will do much to foster a climate that is conducive to generativity and supportive of the changing needs of faculty as they encounter the challenges of their careers and move through the seasons of their lives.

The changes higher education has experienced in the last decade will be dwarfed by the changes sure to occur . . .

BIBLIOGRAPHY

The ERIC Clearinghouse on Higher Education abstracts and indexes the current literature on higher education for the National Institute of Education's monthly bibliographic journal *Resources in Education*. Most of these publications are available through the ERIC Document Reproduction Service (EDRS). Publications cited in this bibliography that are available from EDRS include the ordering number and price at the end of citation. Readers who wish to order a publication should write to the ERIC Document Reproduction Service, P.O. Box 190, Arlington, Virginia 22210. When ordering, please specify the document number. Documents are available as noted in microfiche (MF) and paper copy (PC).

American Council on Education. *Higher Education & National Affairs*, October 15, 1982.

Andrews, John D. W. "Growth of a Teacher." *Journal of Higher Education* 49(March/April 1978):136–50.

Armstrong, Forrest H. "Faculty Development Through Interdisciplinarity." *Journal of General Education* 32(Spring 1980):52–63.

Baker, Frank, ed. *Organizational Systems: General Systems Approaches to Complex Organizations*. Homewood, Ill.: Richard D. Irwin, 1973.

Bakker, Gerald R., et al. *Professional Development of Faculty: Criteria for Evaluation, Support, and Recognition of College Teachers*. Center for Research on Learning and Teaching 4. Ann Arbor: Michigan University Press (March 1977). ED 138 207. MF-$1.17; PC-$3.70.

Baldwin, Roger. "Adult Career Development: What Are the Implications for Faculty?" *Current Issues in Higher Education*, no. 2, pp. 13–20. "Faculty Career Development." Washington, D.C.: AAHE, 1979. ED 193 998. MF-$1.17; PC not available EDRS.

―――. "Fostering Faculty Vitality: Options for Institutions and Administrators." *AAUP/ERIC Administrative Update* 4(Fall 1982). ED 220 069, MF-$1.17; PC-$3.70.

Baldwin, Roger; Brakeman, Louis; Edgerton, Russell; Hagberg, Janet; and Maher, Thomas. *Expanding Faculty Options: Career Development Projects at Colleges and Universities*. Washington, D.C.: AAHE, 1981. ED 217 780. MF-$1.17; PC not available EDRS.

Bergquist, William H., and Phillips, S. R. "Components of an Effective Faculty Development Program." *Journal of Higher Education* 46(March/April 1975):177–221.

Bess, James L. "Integrating Faculty and Student Life Cycles." *Review of Educational Research* 43(Fall 1973):337–403.

―――. "The Motivation to Teach." *Journal of Higher Education* 43(May/June 1977):243–58.

———. *Motivating Professors to Teach Effectively*. New Directions for Teaching and Learning, no. 10. San Francisco: Jossey-Bass, 1982.

Blackburn, Robert T. "Academic Careers: Patterns and Possibilities." *Current Issues in Higher Education*, no. 2, pp. 25–27. Washington, D.C.: AAHE, 1979. ED 193 998. MF-$1.17; PC not available EDRS.

Blake, J. Herman, and Sanfley, R. W. *A Case Study in Faculty Development in Individualizing the System*. San Francisco: Jossey-Bass, 1976.

Brookes, M. C. T. "Generativity, Stuckness, and Insulation: Community College Faculty in Massachusetts." Doctoral dissertation, University of Massachusetts, 1980.

Buhler, Charlotte. "The Curve of Life as Studies in Biographies." *Journal of Applied Psychology* 19(1933):405–09.

Carnegie Commission on Higher Education. *Toward A Learning Society: Alternative Channels to Life, Work, and Service*. New York: McGraw-Hill, 1973.

Carnegie Council on Policy Studies in Higher Education. *Three Thousand Futures: The Next Twenty Years for Higher Education*. San Francisco: Jossey-Bass, 1980. ED 183 076. MF-$1.17; PC not available EDRS.

Carnegie Fund's Report on Academic Governance. *Chronicle of Higher Education*, October 13, 1982, pp. 10, 12–13.

Centra, John A. "Pluses and Minuses for Faculty Development." *Change* 9(December 1977):47–48, 64.

———."Types of Faculty Development Programs." *Journal of Higher Education* 49(1978):151–62.

———."Faculty Development in Higher Education." *Teachers' College Record* 80(September 1978):188–201.

Chait, R. P., and Gueths, J. "Proposing a Framework for Faculty Development." *Change* 13(May/June 1981):30–33.

Cohen, Arthur M. "Toward a Professional Faculty." In *Toward a Professional Faculty* edited by Arthur M. Cohen, pp. 101–17. New Directions for Community Colleges, no. 1. San Francisco: Jossey-Bass, 1973.

Cohen, Arthur M., and Brawer, F. B. *The Two-Year College Instructor Today*. New York: Holt-Rinehart, 1977.

Cole, Charles C. *To Improve Instruction*. AAHE-ERIC Higher Education Research Report no. 2. Washington, D.C.: AAHE, 1978. ED 153 583. MF-$1.17; PC-$7.58.

Croy, John E. "How Do You Feel About In-Service Programs?" *Community and Junior College Journal* 44(November 1973):28–29.

Davitz, Joel, and Davitz, L. *Making It From 40 to 50*. New York: Random House, 1976.

Developing Faculty Careers

Drucker, Peter. *The Age of Discontinuity*. New York: Harper & Row, 1969.

———. *Adventures of a Bystander*. New York: Harper & Row, 1979.

Eble, Kenneth E. *The Art of Administration*. San Francisco: Jossey-Bass, 1978.

Erikson, Erik H. *Childhood and Society*. New York: W. W. Norton, 1950.

Erikson, Erik H., ed. *Adulthood*. New York: W. W. Norton, 1978.

Erikson, Erik H., and Erikson, Joan. "On Generativity and Identity: From A Conversation with Erik and Joan Erikson." *Harvard Educational Review* 51(May 1981):249–69.

Eugen, T. L. "Mid-Career Changes: Self-Selected or Externally Mandated." *Vocational Guidance Quarterly* 25(June 1977):320–28.

Fenker, R. M. "The Incentive Structure of a University." *Journal of Higher Education* 48(1977):453–71.

Ferguson, Marilyn. *The Aquarian Conspiracy: Personal and Social Transformation in the 1980's*. Los Angeles: J. P. Tarcher, Inc., 1980.

Ferren, Ann S., and White, L. G. "Models for Faculty Development." *Teaching Political Science* 5(October 1977):23–28.

Freedman, Mervin; Brown, Wendy; Norbert, Ralph; Shukraft, Robert; Bloom, Michael; and Sanford, Nevitt. *Academic Culture and Faculty Development*. Berkeley, Calif.: Montaigne Press, 1979.

Friedlander, Jack. "The Relationship Between General Job Satisfaction and Specific Work-Activity Satisfaction of Community College Faculty." *Community and Junior College Research Quarterly*, no. 2 (April/June 1978):227–39.

Furniss, W. Todd. *Reshaping Faculty Careers*. Washington, D.C.: American Council on Education, 1981.

———. "Reshaping Faculty Careers." *Change* 13(October 1981):38–57.

Gaff, Jerry G. *Toward Faculty Renewal: Advances in Faculty, Instructional, and Organizational Development*. San Francisco: Jossey-Bass, 1975.

———. *Faculty Development: The State of the Art in Individualizing the System*. San Francisco: Jossey-Bass, 1976.

Gaff, Sally S.; Festa, C.; and Gaff, J. G. *Professional Development: A Guide to Resources*. New Rochelle, N.Y.: Change Magazine Press, 1978.

Geis, George L., and Smith, R. "Professors' Perceptions of Teaching and Learning: Implications for Faculty Development." Seventh International Conference on Improving University Teaching, 17 July 1981, in Tsukuba, Japan. ED 172 625. MF-$1.17; PC-$3.70.

Gleazer, Edmund J., Jr. "After the Boom . . . What Now for the Community Colleges?" *Community and Junior College Journal* 44(December/January 1974):6–11.

Gould, Roger L. *Transformations: Growth and Change in Adult Life*. New York: Simon and Schuster, 1978.

Grant, W. Vance, and Lind, C. G. *Digest of Educational Statistics, 1977–78*. Washington, D.C.: U.S. Government Printing Office, 1978. ED 157 164. MF-$1.17; PC not available EDRS.

Group for Human Development in Higher Education. *The Faculty Development in a Time of Retrenchment*. New Rochelle, N.Y.: Change Magazine Press, 1974.

Guzzetta, D. J. "Education's Quiet Revolution—Changes and Challenges." *Change* 14(September 1982):10–11, 60.

Hall, Douglas T. "A Theoretical Model of Career Sub-Identity Development in Organizational Settings." *Organizational Behavior and Human Performance* 3(1968):12–35.

———. *Careers in Organizations*. The Goodyear Series in Management and Organizations. Santa Monica, Calif.: Goodyear Publishing Co., 1976.

Hall, D. T., and Nougaim, K. "An Examination of Maslow's Need Hierarchy in an Organizational Setting." *Organizational Behavior and Human Performance* 3(1968):12–35.

Hammons, James O., ed. *Proceedings: The Conference on Questions and Issues in Planning Community College Staff Development Programs*, July 1–3, 1974. The Pennsylvania State University, University Park: Center for the Study of Higher Education, 1975. ED 111 462. MF-$1.17; PC-$16.72.

Hammons, James O., and Jaggard, S. "An Assessment of Staff Development Needs." *Community and Junior College Journal* 47(November 1976):20–21.

Hammons, James O., et al. *Staff Development in the Community College: A Handbook*. Los Angeles: University of California, Clearinghouse for Junior Colleges, 1978. ED 154 887. MF-$1.17; PC-$7.20.

Hammons, James O., and Hunter, W. "Using Consultants to Improve Instruction." In *Changing Instructional Strategies*, edited by James O. Hammons, pp. 37–43. New Directions for Community Colleges, no. 17. San Francisco: Jossey-Bass, 1977.

Harmon, W. W. *An Incomplete Guide to the Future*. New York: W. W. Norton, 1979.

Heald, J. E. "Mid-Life Career Influence." *Vocational Guidance Quarterly* 25(June 1977):309–12.

Hodgkinson, H. L. "Adult Development: Implications for Faculty and Administrators." *Educational Record* 55(Fall 1974):263–74.

Hruska, Elizabeth C. "A Study of Role Perceptions of Faculty at the University of Massachusetts, Amherst." Doctoral dissertation, University of Massachusetts, 1975.

———. "Faculty Development On A Shoestring." Mimeographed. Beverly, Mass.: North Shore Community College, 1980.

Jencks, C., and Riesman, D. *The Academic Revolution*. New York: Anchor Books, Doubleday, 1969.

Kanter, Rosabeth. *Men and Women of the Corporation*. New York: Basic Books, 1977.

———. "Changing the Shape of Work: Reform in Academe." *Current Issues in Higher Education*, no. 1, pp. 3–9. "Perspectives on Leadership." Washington, D.C.: AAHE, 1979. ED 193 997. MF-$1.17; PC not available EDRS.

Kastner, Harold H., Jr. "A System-Wide Approach." *Community and Junior College Journal* 3(November 1973):14–15.

Knapper, Christopher K., ed. "Expanding Learning Through New Communications Technologies." In *New Directions for Teaching and Learning*, no. 9. Kenneth E. Eble and John F. Noonan, editors in chief. San Francisco: Jossey-Bass, March 1982.

Krannich, R. L., and Banis, W. J. *Moving Out of Education: The Educator's Guide to Career Management and Change*. Chesapeake, Va.: Progressive Concepts, Inc., 1981.

Ladd, Everett C., Jr. "The Work Experience of American College Professors: Some Data and an Argument." Paper presented at the National Conference on Higher Education, 17 April 1979, in Washington, D.C. ED 184 406. MF-$1.17; PC-$5.45.

Levey, Robert. "Higher Education Outlook Grim." *Boston Globe*, October 20, 1982, pp. 20–21.

Levinson, Daniel J., et al. *The Seasons of a Man's Life*. New York: Alfred A. Knopf, 1978.

Lewis, Danyl R., and Becker, W. E., Jr., eds. *Academic Rewards in Higher Education*. Cambridge, Mass.: Ballinger, 1979.

Light, W. D., Jr.; Marsden, L. R.; and Carl, T. C. *The Impact of the Academic Revolution on Faculty Careers*. AAHE-ERIC Higher Education Research Report no. 10. Washington, D.C.: American Association for Higher Education, 1973. ED 072 758. MF-$1.17; PC-$9.33.

London, Howard B. *The Culture of a Community College*. New York: Praeger, 1978.

Maeroff, Gene. "Faculty Life Is Changed by Plight of Courses." *New York Times*, March 8, 1982, p. A15.

Magarrell, Jack. "Decline in Faculty Morale Laid to Governance Role, Not Salary: Involvement in College Planning Deemed a Major Factor." *Chronicle of Higher Education*, November 10, 1982, pp. 1, 28.

McGrath, E. J. "Characteristics of Outstanding College Teachers." *Journal of Higher Education* 33(March 1962):148–52.

Minter, W. John, and Bowen, H. R. "Colleges' Achievements in Recent Years Came Out of the Hides of Professors: Minter-Bowen Report, Part II." *Chronicle of Higher Education*, May 19, 1982, pp. 7–8.

Mortimer, Kenneth P., and McConnell, T. R. *Sharing Authority Effectively*. San Francisco: Jossey-Bass, 1978.

National Education Association. "The Pressure-Cooker World of the Teacher." *N.E.A. Reporter*, October 1979.

National Institute of Education. *About the Faculty: A Brief Highlighting of Important Literature Since 1971 on Faculty Characteristics, Attitudes, Satisfaction, Preparation, Evaluation, and Collective Bargaining*. Washington, D.C.: NIE, 1976. ED 125 702. MF-$1.17; PC-$5.45.

Newman, F., Task Force Chairman. *Report on Higher Education*. U.S. Department of Health, Education, and Welfare. Washington, D.C.: U.S. Government Printing Office, 1971. ED 049 718. MF-$1.17; PC-$12.83.

Nichols, David A. "Can 'Theory Z' Be Applied to Academic Management?" Point of View, *Chronicle of Higher Education*, September 1, 1982, p. 72.

O'Banion, Terry. *Teachers for Tomorrow: Staff Development in the Community-Junior College*. Tucson: University of Arizona Press, 1972.

―――. "Staff Development: Priorities for the Seventies." *Community and Junior College Journal* 43(October 1972): 10–11.

―――. *Faculty Development in a Time of Retrenchment*. New York: Change Magazine Press, 1974.

―――. *Organizing Staff Development Programs That Work*. Washington, D.C.: American Association of Community and Junior Colleges, 1978. ED 164 023. MF-$1.17; PC not available EDRS.

O'Connell, W. R., and Meeth, L. R. *Evaluating Teaching Improvement Programs*. New York: Change Magazine Press, 1978.

Owens, Richard E. "Elevating the Importance of Teaching, National Project III, Final Report." Manhattan: Kansas State University, September 1977, p. 17. ED 160 016. MF-$1.17; PC-$3.70.

Parsons, Michael H. ". . . Against the Dying of the Light: Staff Development Confronts the 1980's." Paper presented at the National Conference on Community College Staff and Organizational Development, 1977, at Zion, Ill. ED 145 881. MF-$1.17; PC-$3.70.

Patton, Carl V. "Mid-Career Change and Early Retirement in Evaluating Faculty Performance and Vitality." *New Directions for Institutional Research* 20(1978):69–82.

Peatling, J. H. "Careers and a Sense of Justice in Mid-Life." *Vocational Guidance Quarterly* 25(June 1977):303–08. ED 160 268.

Pezzullo, Diane, compiler. *About Staff Development: A Brief Highlighting of Important Literature Since 1970 on Community Staff Development*. Los Angeles: University of California, Clearinghouse for Junior Colleges, 1978. ED 158 794. MF-$1.17; PC-$5.45.

Pollack, S. *Alternative Careers for Teachers*. Harvard, Mass.: The Harvard Common Press, 1979.

Ralph, Norbet B. "Faculty Development: A Stage Conception." *Improving College and University Teaching* 26(Winter 1978):61–63, 66.

Rice, R. E. "Recent Research on Adults and Careers: Implications for Equity, Planning, and Renewal." A study paper commissioned by the National Institute of Education, December 1979. Mimeographed.

Satin, M. *New Age Politics: Healing Self and Society.* New York: Dell Publishing Company, 1979.

Scott, R. K. "Management's Dilemma: To Train or Not to Train People." *Training and Development Journal* 32 (February 1978):3–6.

Sheehy, G. *Passages: Predictable Crises of Adult Life.* New York: Bantam Books, 1977.

———. *Pathfinders.* New York: William Morrow and Company, Inc., 1981.

Shulman, Carol H. *Old Expectations: New Realities: The Academic Profession Revisited.* AAHE-ERIC Higher Education Research Report no. 2. Washington, D.C.: AAHE, 1979. ED 169 874. MF-$1.17; PC-$7.20.

Skinner, Wickham. "Big Hat, No Cattle: Managing Human Resources." *Harvard Business Review* 59(September/October 1981):106–14.

Smart, John C. "Diversity of Academic Organizations: Faculty Incentives." *Journal of Higher Education* 49(1978):403–19.

Smelser, Neal J., and Content, R. *The Changing Academic Market: General Trends and Berkeley Case Study.* Berkeley, Calif.: University of California Press, 1980.

Smith, Albert B. *Faculty Development and Evaluation in Higher Education.* AAHE-ERIC Higher Education Research Report no. 8. Washington, D.C.: AAHE, 1976. ED 132 891. MF-$1.17; PC-$9.33.

———. "Evaluating Staff Development Programs." In *Developing Staff Potential*, edited by Terry O'Banion, pp. 91–101. New Directions for Community Colleges, No. 19. San Francisco: Jossey-Bass, 1977.

Springob, H. K.; Johnson, J. M.; and Mackwer, L. B. "A Faculty Attitude Survey on Alternate Careers." A paper prepared by the Center for the Management of Organizational Resources at Stevens Institute of Technology, Hoboken, N.J.

Stordahl, Barbara. "Faculty Development: A Survey of the Literature of the 70's." AAHE/ERIC Higher Education Research Currents. Washington, D.C.: AAHE/ERIC, March 1981. ED 200 119. MF-$1.17; PC-$3.70.

Sudano, Gary R. "Teaching: The First 25 Years Are the Hardest." *Chronicle of Higher Education*, September 2, 1982, p. 72.

Super, Donald E. *The Psychology of Careers*. New York: Harper, 1957.

———. "Vocational Development Theory: Persons, Positions and Processes." *Counseling Psychologist* 1(1969):2–9.

———. "Vocational Development Theory in 1988: How Will It Come About?" *Counseling Psychologist* 1(1969):9–13.

———. "Vocational Maturity in Mid-Career." *Vocational Guidance Quarterly* 25(June 1977):294–301.

———. "A Life-Span, Life-Space Approach to Career Development." *Journal of Vocational Behavior* 16(1980):282–98.

Super, Donald E., and Kidd, J. M. "Vocational Maturity in Adulthood: Toward Turning a Model into a Measure." *Journal of Vocational Behavior* 14(1979):255–70.

Toombs, William. "Evaluation and Staff Development Programs." In *Proceedings: The Conference on Questions and Issues in Planning Community College Staff Development Programs*, edited by James O. Hammons. The Pennsylvania State University, University Park: Center for the Study of Higher Education, 1975.

———. "Planning a Program for Faculty Career Change." The Pennsylvania State University, University Park: Center for the Study of Higher Education, January 1978. Mimeographed.

Trumble, R. R. "Young Investigators: Concerns, Options and Opportunities." *Research in Higher Education* 12(1980):335–45.

Tuckman, Howard P. "The Academic Reward Structure in Higher Education." In *Academic Rewards in Higher Education*, edited by Danyl R. Lewis and W. E. Becker, Jr., pp. 165–90. Cambridge, Mass.: Ballinger, 1979.

Vaitenas, R., and Wiener, Y. "Developmental, Emotional, and Interest Factors in Voluntary Mid-Career Change." *Journal of Vocational Behavior* 11(1977):291–304.

Vermilye, Dycman, W., ed. *Individualizing the System*. AAHE/Jossey-Bass Series in Higher Education. San Francisco: Jossey-Bass, 1976.

Vincent, William E. "Locked In and Locked Out." *Community and Junior College Journal* 50(February 1980):54–55.

Wallace, Terry H. "Community College Staff Development: An Annotated Bibliography." The Pennsylvania State University, University Park: Center for the Study of Higher Education, April 1975.

Wattenbarger, James L., and Carpenter, R. S. "Faculty Development: Let Teachers Take the Initiative." *Community College Review* 3(June 1975):25–30.

Wurster, Stephen H., and McCartney, J. F. "Faculty Development: Planning for Individual and Institutional Renewal." *Planning for Higher Education* 9(December 1980):14–21.

ASHE-ERIC Higher Education Research Reports

Starting in 1983 the Association for the Study of Higher Education assumed cosponsorship of the Higher Education Research Reports with the ERIC Clearinghouse on Higher Education. For the previous 11 years ERIC and the American Association for Higher Education prepared and published the reports.

Each report is the definitive analysis of a tough higher education problem, based on a thorough research of pertinent literature and institutional experiences. Report topics, identified by a national survey, are written by noted practitioners and scholars with prepublication manuscript reviews by experts.

Ten monographs in the ASHE-ERIC Higher Education Research Report series are published each year, available individually or by subscription. Subscription to 10 issues is $50 regular; $35 for members of AERA, AAHE, and AIR; $30 for members of ASHE. (Add $7.50 outside U.S.)

Prices for single copies, including 4th class postage and handling, are $6.50 regular and $5.00 for members of AERA, AAHE, AIR, and ASHE. If faster first-class postage is desired for U.S. and Canadian orders, add $.60; for overseas, add $4.50. For VISA and Mastercharge payments, give card number, expiration date and signature. Orders under $25 must be prepaid. Bulk discounts are available on orders of 25 or more of a single title. Order from the Publications Department, Association for the Study of Higher Education, One Dupont Circle, Suite 630, Washington, D.C. 20036, (202) 296-2597. Write for a complete list of Higher Education Research Reports and other ASHE and ERIC publications.

1981 Higher Education Research Reports

1. Minority Access to Higher Education
   Jean L. Preer
2. Institutional Advancement Strategies in Hard Times
   Michael D. Richards and Gerald Sherratt
3. Functional Literacy in the College Setting
   Richard C. Richardson, Jr., Kathryn J. Martens, and Elizabeth C. Fisk
4. Indices of Quality in the Undergraduate Experience
   George D. Kuh
5. Marketing in Higher Education
   Stanley M. Grabowski
6. Computer Literacy in Higher Education
   Francis E. Masat
7. Financial Analysis for Academic Units
   Donald L. Walters
8. Assessing the Impact of Faculty Collective Bargaining
   J. Victor Baldridge, Frank K. Kemerer, and Associates

9. Strategic Planning, Management, and Decision Making
   Robert G. Cope
10. Organizational Communication in Higher Education
    Robert D. Gratz and Philip J. Salem

1982 Higher Education Research Reports

1. Rating College Teaching: Criterion Studies of Student Evaluation-of-Instruction Instruments
   Sidney E. Benton
2. Faculty Evaluation: The Use of Explicit Criteria for Promotion, Retention, and Tenure
   Neal Whitman and Elaine Weiss
3. The Enrollment Crisis: Factors, Actors, and Impacts
   J. Victor Baldridge, Frank R. Kemerer, and Kenneth C. Green
4. Improving Instruction: Issues and Alternatives for Higher Education
   Charles C. Cole, Jr.
5. Planning for Program Discontinuance: From Default to Design
   Gerlinda S. Melchiori
6. State Planning, Budgeting, and Accountability: Approaches for Higher Education
   Carol E. Floyd
7. The Process of Change in Higher Education Institutions
   Robert C. Nordvall
8. Information Systems and Technological Decisions: A Guide for Non-Technical Administrators
   Robert L. Bailey
9. Government Support for Minority Participation in Higher Education
   Kenneth C. Green
10. The Department Chair: Professional Development and Role Conflict
    David B. Booth

1983 Higher Education Research Reports

1. The Path to Excellence: Quality Assurance in Higher Education
   Laurence R. Marcus, Anita O. Leone, and Edward D. Goldberg
2. Faculty Recruitment, Retention, and Fair Employment: Obligations and Opportunities
   John S. Waggaman
3. Meeting the Challenges: Developing Faculty Careers
   Michael C. T. Brookes and Katherine L. German